George Washington's ENGINEER

How Rufus Putnam Won the Siege of Boston without Firing a Shot

WASHINGTON
The Man in Charge

PUTNAM
The Man with the Plan

HEATH
The Man with the Book

KNOX
The Man with the Cannons
(...and oxen...and wagons...)

MIFFLIN
The Man with the Wood
(...and twigs...and twine...)

HOWE
The Man Who Left
(...with troops...and ships...)

by Darcy Pattison, illustrated by Terry Kole

George Washington's Engineer: How Rufus Putnam Won the Siege of Boston without Firing a Shot
by Darcy Pattison
Illustrated by Terry Kole

Text © 2023 Darcy Pattison
Illustration © 2023 Mims House

Mims House
1309 Broadway
Little Rock, AR 72202

MimsHouseBooks.com

Publisher's Cataloging-in-Publication data

Names: Pattison, Darcy, author. } Kole, Terry, illustrator.
Title: George Washington's engineer: how Rufus Putnam won the siege of Boston without firing a shot / by Darcy Pattison; illustrated by Terry Kole.
Description: Little Rock, AR: Mims House, 2023. } Summary: In January 1776, George Washington had a problem: the British army controlled Boston. The colonial army needed to force the British to leave. Washington's solution: ask his engineer Rufus Putnam to help.
Identifiers: ISBN: 978-1-62944-220-4 (hardcover) } 978-1-62944-221-1 (paperback) } 978-1-62944-222-8 (ebook) } 978-1-62944-223-5 (audio) }
LCCN: 2022917191
Subjects: LCSH Putnam, Rufus, 1738-1824--Juvenile literature. } Washington, George, 1732-1799--Juvenile literature. } Generals--Massachusetts--Juvenile literature. } Military engineers--Juvenile literature. } United States--History--Revolution, 1775-1783--Juvenile literature. } Boston (Mass.)--History--Siege, 1775-1776--Juvenile literature. } BISAC JUVENILE NONFICTION / History / United States / Colonial & Revolutionary Periods } JUVENILE NONFICTION / History / Military & Wars } JUVENILE NONFICTION / Science & Nature / History of Science } JUVENILE NONFICTION / Technology / How Things Work-Are Made
Classification: LCC E241.B9 .P38 2022 } DDC 973.3/312/092--dc23

NOTE Many locations names have changed since 1775, and people at that time sometimes spelled words differently. For example, in documents of the time period, Lechmere Point is also called Leachmor Point or Leachmoors Point. We have used Putnam's spelling whenever possible, or spelling from maps of the time period.

DEDICATION

For Pvt. Henry Foster, my father, who bravely served during World War II, to give freedom to a new generation.—Darcy Pattison
To my hubby Bill with appreciation for all the encouragement on this journey.—Terry Kole

During January 1776, General George Washington, commander in chief of the Continental Army, worried about walls and hills. Could they help him drive the British out of Boston?

Battles during the summer of 1775 had forced the British soldiers to retreat to their garrisons in Charlestown and Boston, where they'd been for eight years. The Battle of Bunker Hill, on June 17, 1775, was fought over who would control the high ground to the north of Charlestown. The British won that battle.

Now the redcoats were besieged, which meant they were stuck in Boston. They couldn't move troops by land.

General Washington and his troops could not attack, because they didn't have enough gunpowder for their guns. A cannon or two would surely help.

Fort Ticonderoga

NEW YORK

VERMONT

So, in spite of winter snows and frigid weather, Colonel Henry Knox traveled north to Fort Ticonderoga, where he found and brought back a couple of cannons.

Well, 59 cannons, to be exact.

So what? Cannons are no good if they just sit around. Washington sent some cannons to Continental strongholds around Boston. But he had plans for the rest.

CONNECTICUT

In early 1776, Washington invited several officers to dine with him at his headquarters. Among the men was Colonel Rufus Putnam, Washington's chief engineer.

After dinner, Washington invited Putnam to tarry. Alone, they discussed the problem of driving the British out of Boston. Washington wanted to place the rest of the cannons on the high ground of Dorchester Heights, to the southeast of Boston. From there, the Continental Army could attack British supply boats coming into Boston Harbor and also have a good shot at Boston itself. He hoped this would give them a strong enough position to make the British leave.

Washington gave his engineer a problem: Build a wall to protect his soldiers even though the ground was frozen to the depth of two feet. Putnam said that it was impossible to make a protective wall in the usual way because a shovel couldn't cut into the frozen ground. When Putnam left Washington, he worried about walls, hills, and frozen ground.

On his way home, Putnam stopped by to pay his respects to General William Heath, who oversaw the training of troops. There on Heath's table lay a book that Putnam had never seen before by British engineer John Muller, *The Attack and Defense of Fortified Places.*

How interesting!

But Heath hated to loan out his books. He and Putnam went back and forth. Finally Putnam convinced Heath to let him take the book. He hoped it would help him solve the engineering problem.

Putnam read the book the next day and saw a French invention, a chandelier. First, you lay down a long plank as a base. Then, put a pole near the ends and brace it so the poles stand upright. The French engineers set chandeliers close together, and then between the chandeliers' posts, they stacked fascinés, or bundles of sticks tied together. Putnam realized it was the perfect way to build protective walls despite the frozen ground.

By February 17, everyone agreed to Putnam's plans to build chandelier walls to protect the soldiers.

Quartermaster Thomas Mifflin had his own problems to solve. He was responsible for finding all the supplies needed for Putnam's walls.

Help!

Mifflin didn't worry about walls, hills, or frozen ground. Instead, he worried about wood, nails, wagons, horses, bales of hay, piles of sticks, twine to tie the sticks into bundles, and lots of men. He needed carpenters to build the chandeliers, men to gather sticks and tie them into bundles, wagon drivers, horses, hay for the horses, and food for the carpenters, wagon drivers, and all the other men. From the surrounding countryside, men and supplies poured in to help the Continental Army force the British out of Boston.

For two days, cannonballs flew like hailstones. The soldiers didn't really care if they hit much. They just wanted to take the attention away from Dorchester Heights.

On the night of March 4, Dorchester Heights lay under a full, bright moon. But the valley was filled with haze that made it hard to see. What providence!

Quiet now! Hay wagons ventured out first, laying a wall of hay bales to protect the next wagons and carts from the British army's view and to muffle the sounds of wheels and horses.

800 men accompanied them as an advance party.

Shhh! If the British heard them, all would be lost.

Then the real work began. 300 wagons and carts unloaded supplies on Dorchester Heights, some making three or four trips. 1,200 men quickly set to work building a wall with the chandeliers and fascines. Each completed section of the wall weighed 700 to 800 pounds.

A solemn silence lay over the work. The British must not hear them!

Finally, horses dragged heavy wagons, bringing cannons up the hill.

When the British woke up on March 5 . . .

...Washington's troops controlled Dorchester Heights.

In two places, Putnam's ten-foot-high walls stretched for 200 feet long. Pointing straight at Boston were many of Knox's cannons.

General Howe, the British general in Boston, said that the Continental army had done more work in one night than his whole army would have done in six months.

At first, General Howe ordered his troops to attack Dorchester Heights.

But a violent winter storm hit late that day, making the attack too difficult.

By the time the storm blew over a few days later, the Continentals had strengthened Putnam's walls even more. General Howe realized the British had lost Boston.

After eight years of occupying Boston, the British left on March 17, 1776.

The Siege of Boston was over!

It was the first major American victory in the Revolutionary War. Never again would foreign troops march through Boston's streets.

Sometimes battles are fought with guns and bravery. But sometimes battles are fought with walls and a good engineer, like Rufus Putnam, who knows how to solve problems.

RUFUS PUTNAM–ENGINEER (1738–1824)

The Miriam and Ira D. Wallach Division of Art, Prints and Photographs: Print Collection, The New York Public Library. "Rufus Putnam" New York Public Library Digital Collections.

Rufus Putnam was born in Sutton, Massachusetts. His father died when Rufus was seven, and he was apprenticed to a millwright. He learned how to care for the machinery of a mill, where wheat was ground into flour.

At nineteen years old, Putnam joined the military as a surveyor, a person who measured, mapped, and studied the land. The army knew that understanding the land—the rivers, valleys, hills, and other features—was key to winning battles. To win, an army might need walls, trenches, floating bridges, clear roads, or high places to install cannons.

Putnam fought in the French and Indian Wars between the British colonists and the French colonists. This war would decide who controlled certain areas of North America.

When Putnam joined the Continental Army, he helped solve the problem of how to safely put troops and cannons on Dorchester Heights. His efforts helped win the Siege of Boston, without firing a shot. Later, he designed military structures to defend New York City.

General Washington and the Continental Congress were busy setting up the country. Putnam wrote to Washington urging the new government to create a corps of engineers to build military structures. He suggested the corps include engineers, carpenters or wheelwrights, smiths, masons, miners (experts in land mines), sappers (experts in trenches and tunnels), and laborers. In 1778, as other engineers joined in the requests, Congress established three companies of engineer troops.

By the end of the war, Putnam was a brigadier general. After the war, Putnam helped form the Ohio Company, which established Marietta, Ohio, in 1788, the first permanent European-American town in the Northwest Territory. Washington appointed him as a judge in Ohio. Influential, he helped prevent Ohio from allowing slavery. Later, he was named the surveyor-general of the United States.

Putnam made a name for himself during the American Revolutionary War as an engineer. Today, his work is carried on by the Army Corps of Engineers. They still help the military, but they also oversee construction of civil projects such as dams, flood prevention, storm damage protection, and restoration of aquatic ecosystems.

SOURCES and CREDITS

Walker, Paul K. *Engineers of Independence: A Documentary History of the Army Engineers in the American Revolution, 1775-1783.* Historical Division, Office of Administrative Services, Office of the Chief of Engineers, 1981, reprinted 1992. (https://www.publications.usace.army.mil/Portals/76/Publications/EngineerPamphlets/EP`870-1-6.pdf). This document includes the full text of Rufus Putnam's memoirs concerning the encounter at Dorchester Heights, along with eyewitness accounts from diaries and letters by: soldier Peter Brown, British general Sir William Howe, General George Washington, John Chester, Jeduthan Baldwin, James Thacher, Rev. William Gordon, Col. Charles Stuart, and engineer Richard Gridley.

Signature on back cover: Simtropolitan, originally by General Rufus Putnam - Digitally traced from The Rutland Home of Major General Rufus, by Stephen C. Earle. https://en.wikipedia.org/wiki/Rufus`Putnam#/media/File:RufusPutnam.svg